¡BOCÓN!

A Full-length Play
by
LISA LOOMER

Dramatic Publishing
Woodstock, Illinois • London, England • Melbourne, Australia

*** NOTICE ***

The amateur and stock acting rights to this work are controlled exclusively by THE DRAMATIC PUBLISHING COMPANY without whose permission in writing no performance of it may be given. Royalty fees are given in our current catalog and are subject to change without notice. Royalty must be paid every time a play is performed whether or not it is presented for profit and whether or not admission is charged. A play is performed any time it is acted before an audience. All inquiries concerning amateur and stock rights should be addressed to:

DRAMATIC PUBLISHING
P. O. Box 129, Woodstock, Illinois 60098

COPYRIGHT LAW GIVES THE AUTHOR OR THE AUTHOR'S AGENT *THE EXCLUSIVE RIGHT TO MAKE COPIES.* This law provides authors with a fair return for their creative efforts. Authors earn their living from the royalties they receive from book sales and from the performance of their work. Conscientious observance of copyright law is not only ethical, it encourages authors to continue their creative work. This work is fully protected by copyright. No alterations, deletions or substitutions may be made in the work without the prior written consent of the publisher. No part of this work may be reproduced or transmitted in any form or by any means, electronic or mechanical, including photocopy, recording, videotape, film, or any information storage and retrieval system, without permission in writing from the publisher. It may not be performed either by professionals or amateurs without payment of royalty. All rights, including but not limited to the professional, motion picture, radio, television, videotape, foreign language, tabloid, recitation, lecturing, publication, and reading are reserved.

For performance of any songs and recordings mentioned in this play which are in copyright, the permission of the copyright owners must be obtained or other songs and recordings in the public domain substituted.

©MCMXCVIII by
LISA LOOMER

Printed in the United States of America
All Rights Reserved
(¡BOCÓN!)

ISBN 0-87129-870-8

IMPORTANT BILLING AND CREDIT REQUIREMENTS

All producers of the Play *must* give credit to the Author(s) of the Play in all programs distributed in connection with performances of the Play and in all instances in which the title of the Play appears for purposes of advertising, publicizing or otherwise exploiting the Play and/or a production. The name of the Author(s) *must* also appear on a separate line, on which no other name appears, immediately following the title, and *must* appear in size of type not less than fifty percent the size of the title type. *On all programs this notice should appear:*

"Produced by special arrangement with
THE DRAMATIC PUBLISHING COMPANY of Woodstock, Illinois"

The Improvisational Theatre Project of the Mark Taper Forum, Los Angeles, first presented ¡BOCÓN! in 1989. The production was directed by Peter C. Brosius and included the following cast:

(In alphabetical order)
ALMA MARTINEZ
KAREN MARUYAMA
ARMANDO MOLINA
IRMA "CUI CUI" RANGEL
LUCY RODRIGUEZ
JAMES TYRONE-WALLACE II
Percussionist — JOHN FITZGERALD

Movement and Choreography .... Miguel Delgado
Sound Design .... Ara Tokatlian
Original Music .... Ara Tokatlian and John Fitzgerald
Set Design....................... Victoria Petrovich
Costume Design .... Lydia Tanji
Mask Design..................... Alfredo Calderón
Assistant Director .... John Wills Martin
Production Manager .... Diane Divita
Technical Director .... Richard Moore
Stage Manager .... Carol Boland
Assistant Stage Manager............... Jaime Vasquez
Properties Supervisor .... Ron Shulem
Assistant to Costume Designer.............. Judy Bloch
Production Assistants .. Julie Chavez and Bernardo Rosa Jr.
Tour Coordinator .... Dana Axelrod
Manager.......................... Elizabeth Harvey

¡BOCÓN!

A Full-length Play
For 6 actors (with doubling)

CHARACTERS

MIGUEL .... "Bocón" (Big Mouth), a storyteller of 12
BORDER GUARD (offstage voice) .... American
THE JUDGE (voice). .... American
ANA .... Miguel's mother
LUIS .... Miguel's father
CECILIA....................... Miguel's aunt, 40s
ROSITA .... her daughter
KIKI .... an old Indian
LA LLORONA .... "The Weeping Woman"
TWO VIEJITAS .... crazy old crones
THE VOICE KEEPER ... an elegant, smooth, smiling fascist
THE VOICE PICKER ..... a slightly touched old woman
CALAVERA........... a skeleton. A nightmare in boots
DUENDE ...... a trickster, short and green, and a coyote
TWO GUARD DOGS .... fierce, but funny

TIME: Anytime there is war, and refugees.
PLACE: A judge's chambers across the U.S. border;
a village in Central America; and a forest in between.

Running time: Approximately 55 minutes.
One flexible set.

BOCON!

AT RISE: *The play opens with a rhythmic spoken piece—an invitation and a challenge to the audience. The actors are in simple white clothes, suggesting a chorus of campesinos. They each have two (straw) sticks which are beaten against each other, against the floor, in the air, or against the sticks of another actor, creating rhythm and movement.*

CHORUS. Imagine a land—
ACTOR 1. ¡Fíjate, imagine!
CHORUS. Jaguars, papagallos—
ACTOR 2. Yellow corn in the fields—
CHORUS. Imagine a land—¡fíjate imagine!
ACTOR 3. ¡Oye marimba!
ACTOR 4. ¿Quieres sandías?
ACTOR 5. ¡Mira—Quetzal en las ceibas allí!
CHORUS. Imagine a place—WAR in the mountains!
ACTOR 1. There's war in the mountains!
ACTOR 2. Fire in the sky!
CHORUS. Imagine this place—not far from here...
ACTOR 3 *(whispered)*. Fíjate, imagine—

(Faster now, imploring.)

ACTOR 1. Cross the borders!

ACTOR 4. Take my story—
CHORUS. Cross the borders—
ACTOR 5. Take my hand!
CHORUS *(fading)*. Take my story, take my story... Fíjate, imagine...

SCENE ONE

SCENE: *Night. The stage is bare and dark. Sound of HELI-COPTERS. MIGUEL enters and begins to run from a Border Guard we do not see. The CHORUS creates a border with their sticks, stopping him. As soon as he speaks, the CHORUS vanishes.*

BORDER GUARD'S VOICE *(out of breath)*. Stop! That's it, kid. Now you hold it right there.

(MIGUEL stops. It is as though a bird were being captured. One of MIGUEL's arms is lifted up, then the other, like wings. Then both are brought down and back behind him, and the chase is over.

The JUDGE appears behind a scrim, or he may be a shadow cast over MIGUEL, or just a voice over a microphone.)

JUDGE. What's your name, son?

(MIGUEL is too frightened and confused to speak.)

¡BOCÓN! 9

JUDGE. Where do you come from? Guatemala? Mexico? El Salvador? *(Waits.)* Who brought you here? Your parents? Where are your parents, son? *(Louder, slowly.)* ¿Sus padres? ¿Dónde estan sus padres? *(Clears throat.)* Look. I am a judge, son. How am I supposed to know where to send you back to, if I don't know where you're from? *(Faster, more insistently.)* What are you afraid of? Where are your parents? WHERE ARE YOU FROM? *(The last line echoes. The JUDGE bangs his gavel—and we hear THE BOOT sound that MIGUEL hears in his mind.)*

SCENE TWO

SCENE: *MIGUEL starts to tell the JUDGE his story, awkwardly at first. As he gets more comfortable, it is directed more and more to the audience.*

MIGUEL. Yo vengo de...es un pueblito... I come from a small village, San Juan de La Paz, in the middle of my country...by the river they call La Ballena—because the river swells up sometimes like a fat green whale! And we—all the people there work for Don Madera, picking his coffee for him in the fields and— *(Remembers, smiles.)* My father says he can't pick his own coffee 'cause his belly is so big, he— *(Sticks belly way out.)* can't find the basket! *(Laughs at his joke—then explains it.)* To put the coffee beans in, pos... *(Embarrassed.)* Bueno, after you're done working, you could go to the Plaza—where there's always people selling... *(From off-*

stage, we hear the VENDORS selling their wares, softly beckoning MIGUEL's memory.)

VENDOR 1 (ROSITA) *(singsong)*. ¡Pupusas!
VENDOR 2. ¡Bananos!
VENDOR 3. ¡Flores!

(They enter and spread out their wares—which are glued to blankets and unfurled, as memory is unfurled, in a swirl of color and movement.)

VENDOR 4 (CECILIA). ¡Tamales!
ROSITA. ¡Aguacates!
VENDOR 3. ¡Piñas!
ROSITA. ¡Manzanas!
VENDOR 2. ¡Aguas frescas!

(MIGUEL takes a bunch of firecrackers from his pocket—a self-styled vendor.)

MIGUEL *(to the plaza)*. Firecrackers! ¡Cohetes! ¡Para La Fiesta de San Juan! The saints love firecrackers—that's how they know there's a fiesta. *(To the sky.)* Saints—come down from the sky, and bring a fat juicy pig for Rosita! ¡Qué vengan a la fiesta—todos los Santos gordos—all the fat saints!
ROSITA. Miguel!
MIGUEL. Come down before Rosita eats all the food in the village!
CECILIA. Ay, he's got a big mouth—
ROSITA *(eating a pupusa)*. ¡Bocón!
MIGUEL. Come sing!

CECILIA. Not so loud, Bocón, or the soldiers will hear you!

(But this makes him more rambunctious—and he sings a rhythmic child's song to which he's changed the words to mock the soldiers.)

MIGUEL *(sings defiantly)*.
 ¡CHANCA BARRANCA, HOJITOS DE LAUREL,
 SOLDIERS OF MY VILLAGE—SOLDADOS DE PAPEL!

CECILIA. ¡Cállate! Quiet!
MIGUEL *(to audience; still giddy)*. The soldiers didn't like us to shout or sing...

(KIKI EL LOCO enters and prepares for his ritual dance.)

MIGUEL *(serious now)*. Or dance.

(The tone of the scene changes, as KIKI is as much a part of the spirit world as this one.)

MIGUEL. But there was an old Indian, Kiki El Loco, who used to dance all the time at fiestas—right in the plaza! They say he was deaf—but he could hear music right through the ground—like a radio!

(KIKI begins to dance. It's part folk dance, part wizardry, part protest. The others watch in awe—and some fear.)

CECILIA. Mira ese Kiki El Loco—how many times have they told him, "Don't dance!"
MIGUEL. He's not afraid of nothing! ¡Mira—the Dance of the Quetzal! The Bird of Freedom! *(We hear the sound of THE BOOT.)* ¡Los Soldados! The soldiers!

(The VENDORS run off, frightened.)

ANA *(calls from offstage)*. Miguel!
MIGUEL *(calls, without moving)*. ¡Sí, ahorita vengo, Mamá! Coming! *(We hear THE BOOT, closer. Fierce whisper from MIGUEL.)* Kiki! ¡Allí vienen los soldados, Kiki! The soldiers!

(KIKI stomps into the ground, defying the soldiers. As he dances off, he gives MIGUEL a magnificent red and green feather. THE BOOT fades.)

MIGUEL *(to audience; with wonder)*. The feather of the Quetzal! The Bird of Freedom... Kiki—he danced the soldiers away. He's not afraid of nothing! *(Sings, fearless.)*
   CHANCA BARRANCA HOJITOS DE LAUREL,
   SOLDADOS DE MI TIERRA, SOLDADOS GO TO—

ANA *(offstage)*. Miguel! Come in now or La Llorona's gonna get you!
MIGUEL *(terrified)*. La Llorona...!

SCENE THREE

SCENE: *ANA runs on and pulls MIGUEL to another part of the stage, and we are in their house. She lays their petates (mats) and blankets on the floor, then begins to wash MIGUEL in a basin, as he continues to the audience.*

MIGUEL. La Llorona! "The Weeping Woman." Everybody in the village says she's a witch. They say—
ANA. She killed her own children! *(ANA is killing MIGUEL's ears, scrubbing.)*
MIGUEL. ¿Verdad, Mamá?
ANA. They say she drowned them in the river! *(She nearly drowns MIGUEL.)*
MIGUEL. ¡Ay, Mamá, por favor!
ANA. And then—was she sorry! She was so sad, she's been going all over the world for hundreds of years crying— *(Bloodcurdling.)* "¡Ay mis hiiiiijos!"
MIGUEL *(wails)*. "My children! My children!"

(ANA gets him under the blankets. The basin is turned over and covered with a cloth, becoming an altar.)

ANA *(scary)*. And if you're outside after dark, she'll think you're one of her children—and she'll grab you and take you down to the river too! *(Her tone changes completely and she's just a regular loving mom. Sweetly:)* Good night, Miguel. *(ANA lies down beside him and sighs, content. Then we hear, in the wind...)*
LA LLORONA'S VOICE *(bloodcurdling)*. ¡Ay mis hiiiiijos!

(The altar shakes. MIGUEL jumps about three feet in the air, startled.)

MIGUEL. Mamá! I saw her! La Llorona—right outside, allí! She was dressed all in black and she was ten feet tall—and she was floating on the air, Mamá! She had a face like death, como la Calavera— *(Makes a deathly face.)* Así! And yellow teeth like a dog—and snakes for hair—and she put a magnet in me— *(Hand to his heart.)* Here! And she was pulling me... Right. Down. To the river. And she was crying, "¡Ay mis hiiiijos!"

ANA *(calmly)*. Cálmate, Miguel. *(She pulls him down beside her on the mat. Shakes her head and sighs, "What a nut." She crosses herself. They go to sleep. Then...)*

LA LLORONA'S VOICE. ¡Ay, mis hiiiijos!

(The house, the mountains—the whole set shakes. ANA and MIGUEL sit straight up, crossing themselves madly.)

ANA *(trying to convince herself)*. It was just the wind, m'hijo, nada más. Duérmete con los ángeles—sleep with the angels, sí? *(She begins a lullaby.)* A la ru-ru niño, a la ru-ru ya... duérmese mi niño...

(LUIS enters.)

LUIS *(gravely)*. Ana— *(ANA goes to him.)* Kiki El Loco has disappeared.

(MIGUEL pops up.)

MIGUEL *(straight out)*. Kiki? He disappeared? *(Cries.)* No!

SCENE FOUR

SCENE: *A ROOSTER CROWS. It is dawn. MIGUEL comes D to the audience.*

MIGUEL. A lot of people were disappearing in my village.

(LUIS sharpens his machete. ANA rolls up the blankets and prepares tortillas, patting rhythmically.)

MIGUEL. But how do people disappear, Papá? Does the earth just open up and suck them in? Or—or maybe it's the duendes, the little green people that trick them into their caves—or one of those ships that come down from the sky!—or maybe it's the—
LUIS *(puts a gentle hand over MIGUEL's mouth).* Soldiers.
MIGUEL *(softly).* I know...
LUIS. Vámanos.

(ANA sprinkles holy water in the four corners of the house and exits. MIGUEL gets his machete and his guitar. He starts to go in the wrong direction. LUIS turns him around.)

LUIS. Norte, Miguel. North. *(They walk, circling the stage, to the fields.)*
MIGUEL. But why are the soldiers so angry with us, Papá? If the soldiers are supposed to protect us, why is everybody afraid of them?
LUIS. It's a long story.

MIGUEL *(to audience)*. A lot of my father's stories were long, but it was a long walk to the fields...

LUIS. When the earth was about your age, there was only one man. Adam.

MIGUEL *(cuts in)*. I know—the guy who ate the apple. And then he said, "This apple is so good I'm going to—"

LUIS *(hand over MIGUEL's mouth)*. "Sell it."

(A line of CAMPESINOS appear U, working the fields in a slow rhythmic movement across the stage. LUIS's story is punctuated by the sound of their machetes. D, LUIS and MIGUEL work too.)

LUIS. Well, God didn't like Adam selling his apples, because they weren't Adam's apples.

MIGUEL *(laughs)*. "Adam's apples—"

LUIS *(gives him a look)*. They were the earth's apples. And God was so angry he took his machete and chopped Adam in three— *(He chops with his machete, illustrating.)*

MIGUEL. Cómo una manzana—

LUIS. Like an apple, sí. And God said, "Adam—I'm going to take your head, Adam, and out of your head I'm going to make the Rich Man. Just a big head—and a pair of hands for grabbing. Then I'm going to take your arms and your back, Adam, and make the Poor Man. And the Poor Man will work the fields to put food in the Rich Man's mouth. *(Pause.)* A ver, qué falta? What's left...

MIGUEL. The foot! Sí! And—and God said, "Adam, I'm going to take your foot, and out of your foot I'll make..."

LUIS. "The soldier. And the soldier will kick the Poor Man to do the Rich Man's work forever!" *(Laughs.)* Y ya, m'hijo, that's the world. *(Beat.)* Pos, Adam forgot that he used to be one man, and all that's changed in thousands of years—is now the soldier's got a BOOT! *(Laughing.)* And a dirty one, too! ¡Y fea y cochina también!

MIGUEL *(frightened)*. Papá, not so loud, Papá—the soldiers will hear you, they'll think you're laughing at them!

LUIS *(laughing)*. But I am— I am laughing at them! Big ugly boot y apestosa, smelly, también! *(Beat.)* But one day, m'hijo, the Poor Man's going to put down his machete... *(Raises his arms.)* and use his arms to tell The Boot, "NO MORE!" ¿Sí?

MIGUEL. Sí, Papá.

LUIS. No más. Eso. Soon. A trabajar...

MIGUEL *(takes the feather from his pocket; tentatively)*. Mira, Papá—

LUIS. The feather of the Quetzal—the Bird of Freedom! Vete—run, Miguel, show your mamá—tell her it's good luck!

MIGUEL *(starts to run)*. Sí, Papá!

LUIS *(exits, singing, chopping with his machete)*.
 BRAZOS PARA TRABAJAR...
 CORAZÓN PARA AMAR...
 SEMILLAS PARA PLANTAR...
 ESTA VOZ PARA GRITAR...

(ANA, CECILIA, and ROSITA appear washing clothes and sheets in the river. The sheets billow in the wind. MIGUEL rushes to ANA.)

MIGUEL. Mira, Mamá— *(But the women are busy talking.)*

CECILIA *(waving an envelope).* Mira, Miguel, we got a letter from my daughter—

ANA. ¡En Los Angeles!

ROSITA. The City of Angels! *(Incredulous.)* She's got two jobs! And she eats everyday!

MIGUEL. Sí, pos— *(Tries to show them the feather.)* mira—

ROSITA. She said all the kids there got BIG MOUTHS—just like you. Everybody in Los Angeles makes a lot of noise!

CECILIA. They got radios in their cars, and they ride around all day in their villages playing music—

ROSITA. LOUD—so the angels can hear them in the sky! And they got radios on their heads—and telephones right in their pockets!

MIGUEL *(laughs; to audience).* What a nut, eh? *(Tries to show ANA the feather.)* Mira—Papá said—

CECILIA. Ay, you could hear your papá laughing all the way to the river. He better be careful—

ANA. He's a brave man, Cecilia.

CECILIA. Brave like Kiki El Loco. Y bocón, Ana, como you know who—

MIGUEL. Sí! Mamá, mira— *(To audience.)* But I never got to show her, porque...

(ANA hears something in the distance and turns U, frightened.)

MIGUEL. My mother wasn't listening, porque... *(Pained; frightened.)* My mother—she can hear a baby cry in the next village—

(We hear THE BOOT, and LUIS is propelled onto the stage by the unseen soldier. His hands are pulled behind him and tied.)

ANA *(running to LUIS)*. No! ¡Déjelo por el amor de Dios! NO, YOU CAN'T TAKE HIM! NO! *(We hear THE BOOT. One of ANA's arms is lifted, then the other. Then both are pulled down behind her by the invisible soldier. We should feel that a bird is being taken. The capture is the same as MIGUEL's in Scene One.)*
MIGUEL *(to audience, with great difficulty)*. And the soldiers took my mother for talking loud, too. And I wanted to scream at them, I wanted to yell— *(He tries to yell— but his voice flies away in terror. We hear his "NOO-OO!" on tape, flying away, echoing, fading. MIGUEL mouths silently, wildly:)* No! No!
ROSITA *(to CECILIA)*. His voice, Mamá—IT FLEW AWAY!

(She runs off scared. ANA and LUIS are taken off, THE BOOT sound dragging them. They recede U, facing the audience.)

ANA. Run, M'hijo, run! I love you...!
MIGUEL *(mouths)*. No!

CECILIA *(grabs MIGUEL and thinks with lightning speed; urgently).* You have to run, Miguel—the soldiers will be back! They'll make you join up with them, or they'll make you disappear—

(MIGUEL shakes his head wildly, "No!" CECILIA takes the envelope from her apron and stuffs it in his pocket.)

CECILIA. Here—take this. A hundred dollars my daughter sent me from Los Angeles. ¡Al norte! ¡Sí! They don't got soldiers there, they got—angels! That's where my daughter went, y tu también, that's where you'll go— *(He starts to run from her. She grabs him; frantic.)* The soldiers don't want us here, Miguel—we're not wanted in our own home! You tell the people in Los Angeles— we just want to work our land in peace! ¿M'entiendes? Speak to me, Miguel—speak! *(Finally realizing.)* ¡Ay, no, por Dios! Your voice—the soldiers scared it away!? *(Hugs him.)* It's hiding m'hijo, it's frightened. You've got to find it. Don't let the soldiers get your voice, Miguel! Don't let it disappear!

(She hugs him and runs off. MIGUEL starts to run all around the stage, through the village. The chorus appears, as VILLAGERS, offering directions as he runs by. If they can unfurl a river or cause a mountain, all the better.)

VILLAGER 1. There's a forest...
VILLAGER 2. Full of dangers—
VILLAGER 3. Then a Border of Lights—
VILLAGER 1. And the City of Angels!

VILLAGER 2. Tell the people there—
VILLAGER 1 *(cries out)*. We got no more angels!
VILLAGER 2 *(imploring)*. Tell our story!
ALL. Tell our story... Tell our story... Tell our story...

SCENE FIVE

SCENE: *MIGUEL runs and runs. When he stops, he's in a strange new world. The forest. All the characters here are masked. He looks around. Suddenly, he hears...*

LA LLORONA'S VOICE. ¡Ay, mis hiiiijos!
VOICES *(offstage, frightened)*. ¡La Llorona... La Llorona!

(MIGUEL has no idea which direction to go. He starts to go in one direction—and a REFUGEE runs by, carrying her house on her back.)

REFUGEE. Not that way—the soldiers!

(He starts in another direction. A DUENDE COYOTE runs on, a short, green, fast-talking trickster.)

DUENDE. Oye, going North? Need a coyote?

(MIGUEL nods. DUENDE spins him.)

DUENDE. Iiiit's... that way! *(Spins him the other way.)* Not that way—*that* way! *(Spins him again.)* No, not *that* that way—THAT WAY!

(The DUENDE runs off with his money. MIGUEL's still reeling. When he checks his money, it's gone. He tries to shout after the DUENDE, but has no voice for his rage. He tries calling his voice, summoning it with his guitar. An old WOMAN enters, making tortillas. We do not see her face. MIGUEL goes to her. Suddenly she turns, rising to her full height—ten feet tall. It's...)

LA LLORONA *(wails)*. ¡Ay, mis hiiiijos! ¡Córrele!

(MIGUEL is too scared to move.)

VOICES *(offstage)*. La Llorona... La Llorona...!
LA LLORONA. ¡Ay, mis hiiijos! Run hoooome!

(MIGUEL looks back towards home. He can't go there!)

LA LLORONA. ¡Ay, mis hiiijos! ¡CÓRRELEEE!

(MIGUEL gathers all his strength and shakes his head "no." LA LLORONA tears off her mask, incredulous. No one has ever refused to run from her. She's completely thrown. In fact, she sounds just like a regular woman.)

LA LLORONA. ¿Oye, tonto, qué te pasa a ti? What's the matter with you? Crazy kid—ay, ay, ay, ay, ay...

(MIGUEL can't believe his eyes and ears.)

LA LLORONA. What does it take to send you home?

(He starts to explain without words.)

¡BOCÓN!   23

LA LLORONA. You can't go home? *(Responding to his gestures.)* You'll DIE if you go home!? *(Responding to more gestures.)* The soldiers took your parents!? *(She bursts into tears. They don't call her "The Weeping Woman" for nothing. There's an elaborate ritual to her crying—a beginning, a build, then an explosion, so that each time we hear it, we know exactly what's coming, and it's increasingly comical. Sputtering through tears:)* I try to scare you kids home, so you'll be safe from the soldiers. *(Incredulous.)* Now you're too scared to go home—'cause there are soldiers there too!?

(MIGUEL gestures, "Please stop crying.")

LA LLORONA. ¿Qué? You think it's easy going all over the world crying— *(Wails.)* "¡Ay, mis hiiiijos!" *(Beat; regular gal.)* Ay, it hurts. My throat's been killing me for a century. I'm up all night scaring children into their houses— I haven't had a good night's sleep in four hundred years! Not since the Conquistadores. Well, who else is gonna do it, eh? *(Waits.)* Oye, say something already or— *(This usually gets 'em.)* I'll drown you in the river!

(MIGUEL mimes "I've lost my voice!")

LA LLORONA. You've lost your voice?

(He gestures about the soldiers.)

LA LLORONA. The soldiers...scared it away?

(He nods. She starts the build to tears—then stops abruptly mid-wail.)

LA LLORONA. No. There's no time. *(Thinks out loud.)* You can't go home... You've got to find your voice— *(Tentative.)* Pues, maybe I could help him... *(The thought terrifies her. After all, she's gone alone for hundreds of years. She paces; to herself.)* Ay, no... Pues, sí... Pues, no... Pues, sí... Pues—just till he finds his voice? Okay. *(Goes to him.)* Óyeme bien. The voices are trapped. Locked up in the Palace of the General. No one can get in. There's a gate of iron—high as the sky. And wild dogs, with teeth as sharp as razors. But the most dangerous of all is the Voice Keeper. He will trick you and trick you—till you forget why you came. Pues—you must not listen to him!

(MIGUEL gestures, "Not me.")

LA LLORONA. Not you, good. Apúrete, pues! And be careful! Show me you can't be tricked and I'll lead you to the Border of Lights!

(MIGUEL starts to go in the wrong direction. She turns him around.)

LA LLORONA. ¡Ay, por Dios—Norte, North—allí!

(She runs off. MIGUEL starts to walk, calling his voice tentatively with his guitar. Two VIEJITAS with creaky voices enter arguing.)

¡BOCÓN! 25

VIEJITA 1. Over that fence, mujer, under the volcano...
VIEJITA 2. No, mujer, in the general's garden—that's where I've heard the voices...
VIEJITA 1 *(noticing MIGUEL).* Why is he playing that guitar for? Dangerous! ¡Peligroso!
VIEJITA 2. He's calling his voice, mujer!
VIEJITA 1. Con la guitarra, mujer? Muy loco! *(To MIGUEL.)* You'll never get behind that gate—
VIEJITA 2. But if you do—
BOTH. Watch out for the dogs!
VIEJITA 1. Los perrrros, sí!

(They go off laughing, howling like dogs. MIGUEL arrives at the palace. He bangs on the iron gate so hard, he hurts his hand. The VOICE KEEPER appears with a metal box full of voices. And two huge guard dogs, one red, one blue.)

VOICE KEEPER *(smooth as silk).* Why all the noise, hermano? The general is sleeping. Sssshhh!

(MIGUEL bangs on the gate.)

VOICE KEEPER. ¡No, no, hermano! You don't want your voice. They're nothing but trouble!

(MIGUEL keeps trying to get through.)

VOICE KEEPER. That's why we keep them locked up— *(Pats box.)* in here. The loud ones. The ones that talk too much. *(Bows.)* I'm the Voice Keeper. I keep things nice and quiet. For the general.

(He salutes in the direction of the palace. MIGUEL bursts through the palace gate. The dogs growl. The VOICE KEEPER tries to seduce MIGUEL with his words.)

VOICE KEEPER. The voices lie, hermano... They tell stories about the general. They get together, one voice starts in—and before you know it, every one of them has an opinion. There's a racket in the garden. The general can't sleep.

(MIGUEL tries to get the box. The VOICE KEEPER sidesteps, doing flamenco.)

VOICE KEEPER. Always complaining... crying "I'm hungry!" Whining, "It's not fair!" Well, that's not our fault. We didn't make the world!

(MIGUEL manages to get the box open for a moment. A MURMUR OF VOICES flies out. The KEEPER closes the lid.)

VOICE KEEPER *(in a rage)*. ¡Infeliz! *(Quickly smiles.)* Óyeme, hermano, the voices are happy now... content. Listen for yourself—

(MIGUEL listens. He hears silence.)

VOICE KEEPER. No more shouting, no more tears... A kinder, gentler garden. *(He takes a shiny medal coin from his sash and starts to hypnotize MIGUEL.)* You don't want your voice, hermano. You don't want to tell bad stories about the general's soldiers... Promise? *(He is inadvertently hypnotizing the dogs too.)* The general loves you, hermanito! You're a good boy... A quiet boy... Good. ¿Sí?

(He teaches MIGUEL a gesture—a "ssshhhh" and a thumbs-up. MIGUEL repeats the gesture, like a dazed, smiling Moonie. The KEEPER waves and gestures, exiting. The good Moonie waves and gestures.

LA LLORONA enters. MIGUEL repeats the gesture to her, smiling dumbly.)

LA LLORONA *("Oh for God's sake")*. ¿Ay mis hijos, qué te pasa a ti? Ay, ay, ay, ay, ay... You give up your fight? For a pretty speech and a smile?

(MIGUEL smiles and does the gesture.)

LA LLORONA. And what will it be like when the whole world is silent? Will you miss the voice of your guitar? The song of the wind—the rain? The sound of your own voice telling the soldier, "¡No! ¿No más"?

(MIGUEL smiles and gestures, thumbs-up, again.)

LA LLORONA. No!? *(She starts to cry. It builds and builds. But again, she catches herself mid-wail.)* No. There's no time. *(Her crying has broken the spell, but good. MIGUEL is MIGUEL. The dogs have awakened as well. Suddenly she hears something.)* Listen! *(He looks at her like she's nuts. She puts her hands to his ears and we hear A MURMUR OF VOICES.) In the wind...the voices are flying away! They're frightened... They're hiding... (Listens.) At the edge of the earth? No— (Listens again.) The Edge of the Sea! (We hear THE BOOT, faintly.)* The soldiers! You've got to find your voice before the soldiers do! Don't let them scare you! *(The dogs growl. She growls back and they run off.)* Oye—show me you can be brave and I'll lead you to the Border of Lights! Apúrete—to the Edge of the Seaaaa!

(He starts to go in the wrong direction. She turns him around.)

LA LLORONA. ¡Al Norte! North! ¡Allí!

(She calls up THE OCEAN, and leaves. We hear WAVES. MIGUEL plays his guitar, calling his voice. Instead, he catches a song.)

VOICE PICKER *(offstage, singing).*
   NONATZIN IH CAUCNIMIQUIZ NOTLE CUILPAN
   XINECHTOCA...

(The VOICE PICKER comes on, caught in, and dragging a large net filled with seaweed, driftwood and shells. She speaks partly to MIGUEL, partly to herself, partly to her shells.)

VOICE PICKER. Sigue, play—I like the old songs... *(Laughs.)* Don't tell the soldiers! *(Searching the stage.)* You heard any voices by here? *(Whispers.)* In the shells—that's where they like to hide. I got a sack full already, but the soldiers won't be happy till I got 'em all. Greedy. And what do they pay me? Beans. *(Laughs crazily.)* Frijoles, sí. Maybe a tortilla.

(MIGUEL follows her, curious.)

VOICE PICKER *(to her net).* Ay, break the back of an old woman. *(Yells at MIGUEL.)* Pos, what else am I gonna do? Find another husband to bring home the frijoles? I had three husbands! *(Rustles her net.)* Dragged off to the wars, all of 'em! Now I got shells. *(Takes one from pocket.)* This one I'm keeping, eh? Listen...

(From the shell we hear the voice of AN AMOROUS MAN. The shell lights up when it speaks.)

VOICE IN SHELL. Ay, mi amor, chula, preciosa, I adore you my love, I want to...
VOICE PICKER *(puts shell back fast).* Don't listen to that. You're too young.

(MIGUEL dives into the net of shells, looking for his voice.)

VOICE PICKER. Oye—stop that! What are you doing? Muchacho feo, mocoso—

(MIGUEL mimes, "I'm looking for my voice!")

VOICE PICKER. You're looking for your voice? Why didn't you say so? Maybe I'll help you... *(Beat; wary.)* Wait a minute—there's a war out there. Which side are you on—our side or their side? *(MIGUEL doesn't know.)* What do you mean, you don't know? Muchacho estupido, tonto... On our side, we look like us, and on their side, they look like them!

(If she has a mask on the back of her head just like the one on the front, maybe in a different color, she can make her crazy point, if not clearer, crazier.)

VOICE PICKER. And even if they look like us—they dress like them, and they pray like them, and they dance like them, and they EAT like them, and we HATE them like them—BECAUSE THAT'S WAR!

(MIGUEL mimes, "I'm like you!" "I'm like you!")

VOICE PICKER *(laughs; arm around him).* You're like me, eh? Good. Good boy... *(Under her breath.)* Y chulo, y precioso también... *(Holds out net.)* Okay. But don't tell the soldiers— *(In case there are soldiers around, she pretends she's being robbed.)* Ay, steal from an old woman, aaaah! *(Sotto; to MIGUEL.)* Just one, eh?

(He picks up a shell—and out flies his voice.)

MIGUEL'S VOICE *(on tape).*
 CHANCA BARRANCA, HOJITOS DE LAUREL,
 SOLDADOS DE MI TIERRA,
 SOLDADOS GO TO—

VOICE PICKER *(laughs wildly).* ¿La voz de un loco, sí? A crazy one!

¡BOCÓN! 31

(MIGUEL holds the shell in the air, thrilled. He tips it and tries to pour the voice down his throat.)

VOICE PICKER. Ay, that's *your* voice? *(To herself.)* He's got a big mouth— *(Suddenly we hear THE BOOT.)* The soldiers! Don't tell the soldiers where you got it! *(Running off.)* Don't say a wooooord!

(She's gone. We hear THE BOOT—and MIGUEL is so frightened, he throws the shell in the air. He dives for it as it falls—but he misses, and the shell shatters on the ground. He tries to catch his voice, but it's flying away, fading. THE BOOT retreats. Silence.

MIGUEL is alone. NIGHT—which could be an actor in black—turns the stage dark. MIGUEL cries, but hears no sound. He touches his cheeks...no tears. He takes the feather of the Quetzal from his pocket and throws it on the ground in despair. Then he plays a line of ANA's lullaby on his guitar to comfort himself.

LA LLORONA enters U, unseen by MIGUEL. She picks up the feather and tucks it in her rebozo. MIGUEL stops playing. It's too painful to remember his mother.)

LA LLORONA. Don't stop. That's a pretty tune. I remember I used to sing it to my own children. After a story...

(He looks at her, amazed.)

LA LLORONA. What? ¿Qué? You think I can't tell a story?

(He shakes his head, "no.")

LA LLORONA. Pues, it's been a long time...three or four hundred years... *(She'd like to comfort him, but she's been scaring people so long, she's afraid herself now to get close.)* Bueno. Eh... Once upon a time... That's how they start, sí?

(He shrugs and walks away.)

LA LLORONA. Well, anyway, once upon a time, there was a boy who lost his voice. And he went aaaall the way to the Gate of the General—and he was very stu— *(Catches herself.)* very brave—but still he couldn't find it. So he went to the Edge of the Sea—and he found his voice! But the soldiers came, and the boy was very scar—

(MIGUEL shakes his head, "no" on "scared.")

LA LLORONA *(corrects herself)*. Very brave... But his voice got scared and flew away. And the boy was very sad, and he cried.

(MIGUEL is very insulted.)

LA LLORONA *(exasperated)*. All right, he *almost* cried. And it was a good thing he didn't, because his voice wasn't lost—it was just trapped somewhere—caught like a bird, waiting for the boy to set it free.

(She gets up and starts to leave. He grabs her leg as if to say, "Wait—what then?")

LA LLORONA. Well, what do *you* think happened? He kept looking—porque—who can live without a voice in this world? Without a voice, you have no story. No one knows where you come from, why you're here. Without a voice, you disappear! Is that what you want?

(He shakes his head, "no.")

LA LLORONA. Okay, it's your story. You find your voice and *you* tell *me* how it ends.

(MIGUEL gestures, "But where do I look?")

LA LLORONA. You must look where you're most scared to go. Even in your darkest dreams. *(Starts to leave again.)* Oye, show me you have the courage to dream... and I'll lead you to the Border of Lights!

(He lies down and tries to dream. But he can't sleep.)

LA LLORONA *(throws up her hands)*. Oh—now he wants a lullaby! Mira, I haven't sung in a couple of hundred years... *(Sighs.)* Okay. *(She clears her throat and starts to sing "La Llorona," the sad song men have sung about her for centuries.)*
  DICEN QUE NO TENGO DUELO, LLORONA,
  PORQUE NO ME VEN LLORAR,
  DICEN QUE NO TENGO DUELO, LLORONA,
  PORQUE NO ME VEN LLORAR—

(In the wind, THE VOICES join in.)

LA LLORONA & VOICES.
>HAY MUERTOS QUE NO HACEN RUIDO, LLORONA,
>Y ES MÁS GRANDE SU PENA...

LA LLORONA *(tiptoes away)*. Go now, m'hijo, to your dreams...

(MIGUEL sleeps. ANA enters U in his dream.)

ANA *(sings)*.
>A LA RU-RU, NIÑO, A LA RU-RU YA...

(LUIS enters, puts down his machete and joins ANA.)

LUIS & ANA *(singing)*.
>DUÉRMESE MI NIÑO...

(A Military Calavera comes up out of the earth, dancing to the lullaby. He's a skeleton in an army jacket and giant boots. He puts a hand over MIGUEL's PARENTS' mouths to silence them. MIGUEL runs to stop him. La Calavera turns on MIGUEL with his machete.)

ANA. ¡No! ¡Déjelo por el amor de Dios!

(MIGUEL grabs a branch and he and La Calavera duel. La Calavera is winning. Just as La Calavera is about to strike a final blow—just as MIGUEL's PARENTS are about to disappear—MIGUEL finds his voice! Pulls it up out of the depths of his own being and sets it free.)

MIGUEL. NO! NO, YOU CAN'T TAKE US! NO, YOU CAN'T STOP US! NO MÁS!

(The fight resumes, and MIGUEL wins! La Calavera goes back down under the earth. MIGUEL's PARENTS raise their arms in slow motion in exaltation. LA LLORONA runs on and shakes MIGUEL, and his PARENTS recede, triumphant.)

LA LLORONA. Wake up now—despiértate, Miguel!

(He comes out of his dream, talking a mile a minute.)

MIGUEL. I did it! ¡Yo gané! ¡Tengo mi voz! My voice! *(Spins LA LLORONA.)* ¡Chanca barranca hojitos de laurel! Vámanos—apúrete—to the City of Angels. Got to tell the people there—we can stop the soldiers! Got to tell our story *loud*—so the angels can hear it in the sky!
LA LLORONA. Ay, he's got a big mouth. ¿Bocón, verdad?
MIGUEL. ¡Bocón! ¡Sí! Ay, what did they tell me? Which way? There's a forest—and then a border. The Border of...

(He's shown her he has the courage to dream. With the wave of an arm, she shows him the Border of Lights. In fact, the entire D area fills with light.)

MIGUEL. The Border of Lights! Ay, look at all those lights! ¡Vámanos! Let's go! *(There is a pause.)*
LA LLORONA *(sadly)*. I can't go with you, Miguel. I can't cross this border.

MIGUEL. ¿Cómo qué no? You can do anything!

LA LLORONA. They don't believe in me up there. *(Beat.)* The only way I can cross is in your heart. *(Practical.)* Besides, I got children to scare all over the continent—

MIGUEL. No lo creo, I don't think you want to scare children—

LA LLORONA. Pues, it's a lousy job, m'hijo, but somebody's got to do it—so they'll run in their houses and be safe from the soldiers! En Guatemala, y El Salvador... y ahora Chiapas, Mexico— *(Sighs; rattles off.)* Y Bosnia, y Ireland, y Rwanda...

MIGUEL *(takes a few steps away)*. Pos, I'm not going to cry—

LA LLORONA. Mira, do the clouds say, "I'm not going to rain"?

MIGUEL *(crying, for the first time in his journey)*. I don't want to go alone.

LA LLORONA *(nods, thinks)*. Pues... listen...

(He listens hard. In the wind, he hears...)

ANA'S VOICE. Miguel! Come in now, or La Llorona's gonna get you!

(MIGUEL and LA LLORONA smile.)

MIGUEL. Mamá—
LA LLORONA. Remember...

(He listens again and hears...)

LUIS'S VOICE. But one day, m'hijo, the Poor Man will raise his arms and tell The Boot, "¡No más!" "No more!"

MIGUEL. Papá!

LA LLORONA. Take them with you. Remember. Like I remember my own children. Porque, when we remember, we keep them alive...and free. Go now. Tell your story.

MIGUEL. Gracias.

LA LLORONA. No, m'hijo, gracias a ti—

MIGUEL. No, pos, a usted gracias—

LA LLORONA. No, no, gracias a ti—

MIGUEL. No, digo, a usted gra—

LA LLORONA *(starts to cry—but catches herself)*. No. There's no time. *(She takes the feather of the Quetzal from her rebozo and hands it to MIGUEL.)* Córrele, m'hijo. Fly!

(Slowly she recedes U, her feet never touching the ground. MIGUEL turns to the Border of Lights and gets it right this time.)

MIGUEL. NORTH!

(He raises his arms in exaltation and, in slow motion, starts to cross the border. We hear the sound of HELICOPTERS. His body goes from exaltation to fear. He starts to run. The CHORUS runs on with their sticks, making the border, as in Scene One.)

SCENE SIX

SCENE: *There is a light change to indicate that we are back in the courtroom where we began. (If the JUDGE appeared behind the scrim in Scene One, he will reappear.) We hear the sound of the GAVEL.*

MIGUEL *(still out of breath)*. And then—and then, señor— a man in a uniform caught me— and took me here.

JUDGE *(chuckles)*. Well. That's quite a story. I've got to hand it to you, son, you kids have some pretty wild imaginations. Things you kids come up with...

(MIGUEL touches the feather of the Quetzal, the rebozo LA LLORONA gave him—both quite real.)

MIGUEL. Señor—Judge, digo—are you going to send me back? *(A pause.)*

JUDGE *(sighs)*. Well, son...thing is, we just don't have a whole lot of room. No room in the playgrounds, no room in the schools...

MIGUEL. But the Border of Lights—it's so bright, it—it puts a magnet in you—

JUDGE. We're turning the lights down, son. Light's expensive—

MIGUEL. Wait! Just—one question, por favor—

JUDGE *(very patiently)*. Yes?

(We hear an echo of the JUDGE's first questions to MIGUEL, "Where do you come from? Where are your parents? Where are you from?")

MIGUEL. Judge... *(Simply.)* Where are you from?

JUDGE *(chuckles; awkward)*. Well, uh... I'm from right here, son. And my parents are from right here, too. And their parents came when they were just children. *(Proud.)* Came from halfway across the world!

MIGUEL *(softly)*. Like me? *(Pause.)*

JUDGE *(caught)*. Well... uhm... uh...

MIGUEL. If you send me home, I'll just come back again. I'm not going to disappear.

JUDGE. I'm sorry, son. *(He bangs his GAVEL. We hear the echo of THE BOOT sound that MIGUEL hears in his mind.)*

MIGUEL. NO! *(MIGUEL stomps into the ground in protest—and up comes a strain of KIKI'S MUSIC.)*

JUDGE. What did you say?

(MIGUEL stomps again—more MUSIC.)

MIGUEL. Kiki—right through the ground like a radio!

(KIKI appears behind the scrim, dancing.)

JUDGE *(mutters)*. Kid's loco!

(In front of the scrim, MIGUEL does a few steps of KIKI's dance.)

MIGUEL. The music—you heard it didn't you?

JUDGE. Nope—

MIGUEL. It followed me! It flew across the border! You can't stop it, señor—it's right here—in my story! And my story's spreading! It's catching— *(Points to girl in audience.)* She's got it, señor, and she's got a BIG MOUTH! *(To girl.)* ¿Una Bocóna, sí? She's going to tell it on the buses, so it rides all over the city! Tell it loud so the ANGELS can hear it! And then— *(We hear the WIND, and in the wind.)*

LA LLORONA'S VOICE. ¡Ay, mis hiiiijos! *(LA LLORONA laughs.)*

MIGUEL. My story's in the wind! *(Yearning.)* It's flying home, Mamá! It's in the plaza and in the fields! It's in the big head of the Rich Man. It's in the arms of the Poor Man, Papá! And he's putting down his machete and he's telling the soldier, "¡No Más!" "No More!" And he's singing... *(MIGUEL sings LUIS's song, translating for the people in his new village.)*

   ¡BRAZOS PARA TRABAJAR—
(Spoken.) Arms to work, eh Papá?
(Sung.)
   CORAZÓN PARA AMAR—
(Spoken.) And a heart to love...
(Sung.)
   SEMILLAS PARA PLANTAR—
(Spoken.) Seeds to plant—
(Sung.)
   ESTA VOZ PARA GRITAR!
(Spoken.) And a voice to cry out and sing—

(The CHORUS comes on and sings the entire song, upbeat now, with MIGUEL, ending with...)

ALL *(singing).*
   ¡CANTA VERSO A VERSO,
   Y BAILA PASO A PASO,

OYE MI BOCÓN—
EL CANTO VOLARÁ!

(The CHORUS finishes with a rhythmic triumphant beating of their sticks. Then ...)

CHORUS. ¡Fíjate, imagine!

END OF PLAY

PRODUCTION NOTES

CASTING

Six actors play all the characters. The actress who plays La Llorona can also play Cecilia. Miguel is usually played by an actor in his 20s.

Ideally, casting should reflect the fact that the main characters are Central American. On the other hand, since Miguel's story happens all over the world, casting is one way to encourage children of other ethnicities to relate to it.

ADDITIONAL CHARACTER NOTES

- MIGUEL: A kid with a wild imagination and reasonable fears in an unreasonable world.
- THE JUDGE: Doing the best he can with the misinformation he's got.
- ANA: Superstitious and loving. One minute she's scaring the daylights out of you, the next she's tucking you in.
- LUIS: Proud and big-hearted, with a great laugh.
- CECILIA: A pragmatist.
- ROSITA: A wild child. Loves to eat.
- KIKI: Part spirit. A wizard of the dance.
- LA LLORONA: The Boogey Woman and Mother Earth. A woman of quick changes, with the stature of a myth and human concerns... and a great comedienne
- THE VOICE KEEPER: Knows flamenco. A Spaniard with a sash of medals.
- THE VOICE PICKER: A raggedy old woman who's caught in a net and talks to shells. She's also caught in the web of war.

THE SET

The set should be minimal, flexible, and evocative rather than literal so it can suggest three different worlds: A courtroom in America; a village in Central America; and a mythical forest which is the setting for an interior journey. The village should be warm and beautiful, like all our remembered homes. The forest can be scarier.

The set might have different levels. The Military Calavera should come up out of the ground. Rope ladders might be used for trees. Especially on the journey, actors need not always be on the ground.

There might be modular, reversible pieces suggesting the topsy-turvy nature of Miguel's world. A set piece might have stars and stripes on one side, an altar on the other, and the face of a wild monkey on the third. Flowing fabric might be used by the actors to create a river. The marketplace might consist of fruits and wares glued to colorful blankets and unfurled.

SOUND AND MUSIC

The original production had a lot of taped music with a distinctly Latin feel. There was a live musician with a variety of ethnic and percussion instruments underscoring and accenting moments throughout the play.

The Judge's voice on mike might have some distortion—because his language is strange to Miguel. The journey is filled with the sounds of the elements and the howling of wild animals. THE BOOT is the sound of oppression. Could be hard as stone, or clanging and metallic like a prison door.

COSTUMES

Because this is a tale, ethnic costumes work well in the village. In reality, Americanized dress might be more common, but the village should feel like a distant world. On the journey, the sky's the limit. The Chorus has worked well in natural cotton, campesino-style shirt and pants.

MASKS

If masks are used, only the characters on the journey should be masked. Masks give a magical lift—but they can also be distancing, so half masks work well. The masks should be achingly human. See Guatemalan and Mexican masks for inspiration. La Llorona's mask should make her huge, ten feet tall, and when she loses it, she's not masked at all.

DIRECTOR'S NOTES

DIRECTOR'S NOTES

DIRECTOR'S NOTES

DIRECTOR'S NOTES